STRUM & SING

Disney

T0071447

The following songs are the property of:

Bourne Co.

Music Publishers

5 West 37th Street

New York, NY 10018

BABY MINE

HEIGH-HO

SOME DAY MY PRINCE WILL COME

WHEN YOU WISH UPON A STAR

WHISTLE WHILE YOU WORK

WHO'S AFRAID OF THE BIG BAD WOLF?

ISBN 978-1-4950-9443-9

HAL•LEONARD®

Visit Hal Leonard Online at
www.halleonard.com

Contact Us:
Hal Leonard
7777 West Bluemound Road
Milwaukee, WI 53213
Email: info@halleonard.com

In Europe contact:
Hal Leonard Europe Limited
42 Wigmore Street
Marylebone, London, W1U 2RN
Email: info@halleonardeurope.com

In Australia contact:
Hal Leonard Australia Pty. Ltd.
4 Lentara Court
Cheltenham, Victoria, 3192 Australia
Email: info@halleonard.com.au

*Based on the "Winnie the Pooh" works, by A. A. Milne and E. H. Shepard
**TARZAN® Owned by Edgar Rice Burroughs, Inc. and Used by Permission. © Burroughs/Disney

Baby Mine
from DUMBO

Words by Ned Washington
Music by Frank Churchill

(Capo 2nd fret)

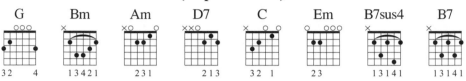

Verse 1

G |Bm |Am | D7 |
Baby   mine don't you cry.

G |Bm |Am | D7 |
Baby   mine dry your eye.

C | |Am
Rest your head close to my heart,

      |D7 |G |Em |Am |D7   ‖
Never to part, baby of mine.

Verse 2

```
G   |Bm          |Am        |       D7 |
Little   one when you play,
G      |Bm          |Am       |    D7 |
Don't you mind what they say.
C      |           |Am
Let those eyes sparkle and shine,
    |D7         |G        |         ||
Never a tear, baby of mine.
```

Bridge

```
Em   |               |B7sus4 |B7       |
If they knew sweet little you,
Em          |               |B7sus4  |B7       |
They'd end up loving you too.
Em        |               |Bm |       |
All those same people who scold   you,
Em        |               |Bm   |Am  D7  ||
What they'd give just for the right  to  hold  you.
```

Verse 3

```
G       |Bm          |Am        |       D7 |
From your head to your toes,
G       |Bm          |Am        |       D7 |
You're not much, goodness knows,
C       |           |Am
But you're so precious to me,
     |D7         |G        ||
Cute as can be, baby of mine.
```

The Bare Necessities

from THE JUNGLE BOOK

Words and Music by
Terry Gilkyson

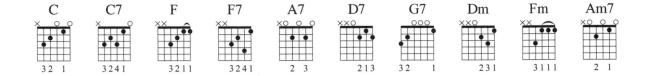

Chorus 1

N.C.   ‖C |C7
Look for the   bare ne - cessities,

   |F |F7
The simple bare ne - cessities;

   |C |A7 |D7 |G7
For - get about your worries and your strife.

     |C |C7
I mean the   bare ne - cessities,

 |F |F7
Or Mother Nature's recipes

   |C   A7 |Dm   G7 |C   F |C
That bring the bare ne - cessities ___ of life.

Verse 1

```
                  ‖G7        |
Wherever I wander,
                |C         |
Wherever I roam,
                  |G7         |
I couldn't be fonder
                |C        |C7
Of my big home.
                |F              |Fm
The bees are buzzin' in the tree
                   |C               |D7
To make some honey just for me.
     |Am   N.C.            |A7   N.C.
When you     look under the rocks and plants
   |Dm   N.C.           |Dm       G7
And take a glance at the fancy ants,
       |C          |A7      |        |        |        |
Then maybe try a few.
|        |        |        |        |
```

```
N.C.          |Dm
The bare ne - cessities
  |G7              |C    A7    |Dm
Of life will come to you,
        G7    |C    F    |C
They'll come to you.
```

Chorus 2

```
N.C.            ‖C            |C7
Look for the     bare ne - cessities,
   |F                |F7
The simple bare ne - cessities;
   |C               |A7              |D7      |G7
For - get about your worries and your strife.
          |C             |C7
I mean the     bare ne - cessities,
     |F               |F7
That's why a bear can rest at ease
     |C    A7      |Dm    G7  |C    F      |C
With just the bare ne - cessities ____ of life.
```

Verse 2

```
N.C.                ‖G7        |
Now when you pick a paw-paw
             |C        |
Or a prickly pear;
             |G7        |
And you prick a raw paw,
             |C           |C7
Next time be - ware.
                 |F               |Fm
Don't pick the prickly pear by the paw,
                 |C              |D7
When you pick a pear, try to use the claw.
  |Am  N.C.           |A7  N.C.
But you   don't need to use  the claw
      |Dm  N.C.              |Dm     G7   |C
When you   pick a pear of the big paw-paw.
               |A7      |        |        |        |
Have I given you a clue?
  |        |        |        |        |

N.C.           |Dm
The bare ne - cessities
  |G7              |C     A7   |Dm
Of life will come to you,
      G7     |C     F   |C   N.C. ‖
They'll come to you.
```

Tuba Solo

```
|C          |C7         |F          |F7        |
|C          |A7         |D7         |G7        |
|C          |C7         |F          |F7        |
|C   A7   |Dm  G7   |C    F   |C   N.C. ‖
```

Piano Solo   ***Repeat Tuba Solo***

Trumpet Solo

```
|C          |C7         |F          |F7        |
|C          |A7         |D7         |G7        |
|C          |C7         |F          |F7        |
|C   A7   |Dm  G7   |C    N.C.  |C   N.C.
```

Verse 3

             ‖ **G7** | |
So just try and   relax, yeah. Cool it.

C |
Fall apart in my back - yard

                    |**G7**
'Cause let me tell ya somethin', Little Britches,

         | |
If you act like that bee acts,

C |**C7**
Uh, ah, you're workin' too hard.

   |**F** |**Fm**
And don't spend your time just lookin' a - round

               |**C** |**D7**
For somethin' you want that can't be found.

    |**Am7 N.C.** |**A7 N.C.**
When you   find out you can live   without it

   |**Dm N.C.** |**Dm**   **G7** |
And go a - long not thinkin' about it.

C |**A7** |
I'll tell you somethin' true.

N.C. |**Dm** |**G7**
The bare ne - cessities of life

            |**C**   **F** |**C** | **F** |**C** |**Dm**
Will come to you,

    |**G7** |**C**   **F** |**C**
Mow - gli, how 'bout you sing.

Chorus 3

N.C.   ‖**C** |**C7**
Look for the   bare ne - cessities,

   |**F** |**F7**
The simple bare ne - cessities;

   |**C** |**A7** |**D7** |**G7**
For - get about your worries and your strife.

     |**C** |**C7**
I mean the   bare ne - cessities,

   |**F** |**F7**
That's why a bear can rest at ease

   |**C**   **A7** |**Dm**   **G7** |**C**   **A7** |**Dm G7**
With just the bare ne - cessities ___ of life.

   |**C**   **A7** |**Dm**   **G7** |**C** | **N.C.**   ‖
With just the bare ne - cessities ___ of life.

Beauty and the Beast
from BEAUTY AND THE BEAST

Music by Alan Menken
Lyrics by Howard Ashman

(Capo 1st fret)

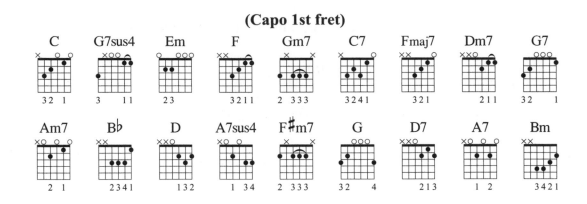

Intro

‖: C | G7sus4 | C | G7sus4   :‖

Verse 1

C | G7sus4 | C
Tale as old as time,

        | G7sus4 | C
True as it can be.

    | Em
Barely even friends,

      | F | G7sus4 | C
Then somebody bends unexpected - ly.

    | G7sus4 | C
Just a little change.

    | Gm7
Small, to say the least.

C7 | Fmaj7
Both a little scared,

   Em | Dm7
Neither one pre - pared.

G7 | C | G7sus4
Beauty and the Beast.

Bridge

```
        ‖ Em    | F
Ever just the same,
        | Em    | F
Ever a sur - prise.
        | Em
Ever as be - fore,
        | Am7              | B♭    C       ‖
Ever just as sure as the sun will rise.
```

Verse 2

```
D                  | A7sus4 | D
  Tale as old as time,
                   | A7sus4 | D
Tune as old as song.
                   | F♯m7
Bittersweet and strange,
                   | G
Finding you can change,
                     | A7sus4   | D
Learning you were wrong.
                   | A7sus4    | D
Certain as the sun
                   | Am7
Rising in the East,
D7             | G
Tale as old as time,
                   | Em
Song as old as rhyme.
A7             | D          | Bm
Beauty and the Beast.
                 | G
Tale as old as time,
                 | Em
Song as old as rhyme.
A7             | D
Beauty and the Beast.
 A7sus4  | D          | A7sus4  | D          ‖
```

Bibbidi-Bobbidi-Boo
(The Magic Song)
from CINDERELLA

Words by Jerry Livingston
Music by Mack David and Al Hoffman

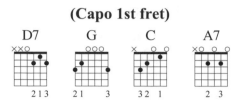

(Capo 1st fret)

D7   G   C   A7

Intro

|D7 | |G | ‖

Verse 1

G | | | |
Salagadoola, menchicka boola, bibbidi - bobbidi - boo.
D7 | |
Put 'em together and what have you got?
           |G   ‖
Bibbidi - bobbidi - boo.

Verse 2

G | | | |
Salagadoola, menchicka boola, bibbidi - bobbidi - boo.
D7 | |
It'll do magic be - lieve it or not,
           |G
Bibbidi - bobbidi - boo.

Bridge

           ‖C | | |G
Now, salagadoola mean, menchicka boole - roo,
           |A7 | |D7 | ‖
But the thingamabob that does the job is bibbidi - bobbidi - boo.

Outro

G | | | |
Salagadoola, menchicka boola, bibbidi - bobbidi - boo.
D7 | |
Put 'em together and what have you got?
           | | |G   ‖
Bibbidi - bobbidi - bibbidi - bobbidi, bibbidi - bobbidi - boo.

Cruella De Vil

from 101 DALMATIANS

Words and Music by Mel Leven

(Capo 4th fret)

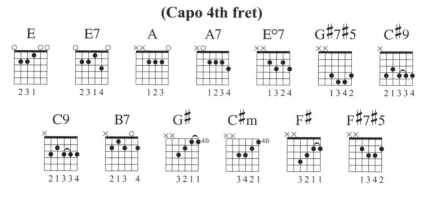

Verse 1

```
‖E        E7      |A        A7      |
```
Cru - ella De Vil, Cru - ella De Vil,

```
|E        E7           |A        A7          |
```
If she doesn't scare you, no evil thing will.

```
|E        E°7          |G#7#5  C#9
```
To see her is to take a sudden chill.

```
|C9       |B7
```
Cru - ella, Cru - ella.

```
|E        E°7          |G#7#5  C#9
```
She's like a spider waitin' for the kill.

```
|C9       B7      |E
```
Look out for Cru - ella De Vil.

Bridge

```
‖G#                   |C#m
```
At first you think Cruella is a devil,

```
|G#                   |C#m
```
But after time has worn away the shock,

```
|F#           |                      |
```
You come to realize you've seen her kind of eyes

```
F#7#5                  |B7
```
Watching you from underneath a rock.

Verse 2

```
‖E     E7    |A        A7
```
This vampire bat, this inhuman beast,

```
|E        E7      |A        A7
```
She ought to be locked up and never re - leased.

```
|E        E°7          |G#7#5   C#9
```
The world was such a wholesome place un - til

```
|C9       B7      |E          ‖
```
Cru - ella, Cru - ella De Vil.

Can You Feel the Love Tonight

from THE LION KING

Music by Elton John
Lyrics by Tim Rice

(Capo 5th fret)

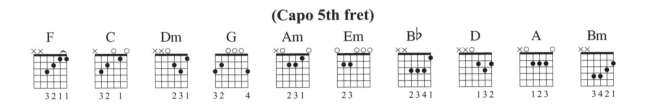

Verse 1

       F   C
I can see what's happ'ning,

        |F   C
And they don't have a clue.

          |F   C
They'll fall in love and here's the bottom line,

         |Dm   G
Our trio's down to two.

         |F   C
The sweet caress of twilight,

          |F   C
There's magic ev'ry - where.

          |F |Am Em F
And with all this ro - man - tic   atmosphere,

         |B♭ |G | ||
Dis - aster's in the air.

Chorus 1

C   G |Am   F |C
Can you feel the love to - night,

           F |G
The peace the evening brings?

 |F   C |Am   F
The world for once in perfect harmony

 |Dm F |G
With all its living things.

Verse 2

‖F   C
So many things to tell her,

 |F   C
But how to make her see

 |F   C
The truth about my past.

        |Dm   G
Impossible!   She'd turn away from me.

 |F   C
He's holding back. He's hiding.

 |F   C
But what? I can't de - cide.

 |F   Am
Why won't he be the king I know he is,

 |B♭ |G | ‖
The king I see in - side?

Chorus 2

C   G |Am   F |C
Can you feel the love to - night,

             F |G
The peace the evening brings?

 |F   C |Am   F
The world for once in perfect harmony

 |Dm F |G   ‖
With all its living things.

Chorus 3

D   A |Bm   G |D
Can you feel the love to - night?

           G |A |G
You needn't look too far.

         D |Bm   G |
Stealing through the night's un - certainties,

Em   G |A
Love is where they are.

Chorus 4

 ‖D A |Bm   G |D
And if he falls in love to - night,

     G |A |G
It can be as - sumed

         D |Bm G
His carefree days with us are history.

 |Em   A |G |D   ‖
In short, our pal is doomed.

Candle on the Water

from PETE'S DRAGON

Words and Music by
Al Kasha and Joel Hirschhorn

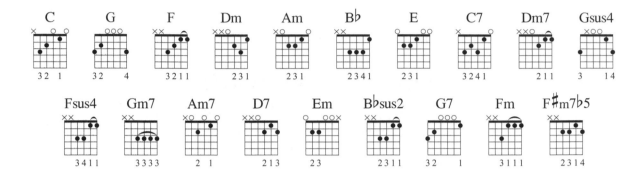

Intro

‖: C   G |F   G :‖

Verse 1

C   Dm |F   G |C
I'll be your candle on the water,

         Am |B♭ G
My love for you will always burn.

  E |Am   C7 |
I know you're lost and drifting,

F   C |
But the clouds are lifting,

F   C |Gsus4 G ‖
Don't give up; you have somewhere to turn.

Verse 2

C   Dm |F   G |C
I'll be your candle on the water,

         Am |B♭ G
'Til ev'ry wave is warm and bright,

  E |Am   C7 |
My soul is there be - side you,

F   C |
Let this candle guide you,

F   C |Gsus4 G ‖
Soon you'll see a golden stream of light.

Bridge

Bb   C7 |Fsus4 F |Bb
A cold and friendless tide has found you,

               C7 |F   Gm7 F |Am7
Don't let the stormy darkness pull you   down.

          D7 |Gsus4 G |
I'll paint a ray of hope a - round   you,

F   Em |F |Bbsus2 |G7 ||
Circling the air,   lighted by a prayer.

Verse 3

C   Dm |F   G |C
I'll be your candle on the water,

              Am |Bb   G
This flame in - side of me will grow.

       E |Am   C7 |
Keep holding on, you'll make it,

F   C |
Here's my hand, so take it,

F   G7 |C
Look for me reaching out to show

    F   Fm |C   F#m7b5 |F
As sure as rivers flow.

   Gsus4 G |C G |F
I'll never let you go,

   G |C G |F
I'll never let you go,

   G |C G |F C G|C | ||
I'll never let you go.

Chim Chim Cher-ee
from MARY POPPINS

Words and Music by
Richard M. Sherman and Robert B. Sherman

(Capo 3rd fret)

Am   E7   Am(maj7)   Am7   D   Dm   B7

Intro

| Am | E7 | Am | E7 ||

Chorus 1

Am |Am(maj7) |Am7 |D
Chim chiminey, chim chiminey, chim chim cher - ee!
 |Dm |Am |B7 |E7
A sweep is as lucky as lucky can be.
Am |Am(maj7) |Am7 |D
Chim chiminey, chim chiminey, chim chim cher - oo!
  |Dm |Am |E7 |Am
Good luck will rub off when I shakes 'ands with you.
 |Dm |Am |E7 ||
Or blow me a kiss and that's lucky…

Interlude

|Am |E7 |Am |E7 ||
 Too.

Verse 1

Am |Am(maj7) |Am7 |D
Now, as the ladder of life 'as been strung,
 |Dm |Am |B7 |E7
You might think a sweep's on the bottom-most rung.
   |Am |Am(maj7) |Am |D
Though I spends me time in the ashes and smoke,
 |Dm |Am |E7 |Am ||
In this 'ole wide world there's no 'appier bloke.

Chorus 2

Am |Am(maj7) |Am7 |D
Chim chiminey, chim chiminey, chim chim cher - ee!
 |Dm |Am |B7 |E7
A sweep is as lucky as lucky can be.
Am |Am(maj7) |Am7 |D
Chim chiminey, chim chiminey, chim chim cher - oo!
 |Dm |Am |E7 |Am ||
Good luck will rub off when I shakes 'ands with you.

Chorus 3

```
Am              |Am(maj7)  |Am7            |D
```
Chim chiminey, chim chiminey, chim chim cher - ee!
```
 |Dm        |Am      |B7      |E7
```
A sweep is as lucky as lucky can be.
```
Am              |Am(maj7)  |Am7            |D
```
Chim chiminey, chim chiminey, chim chim cher - oo!
```
  |Dm          |Am       |E7            |Am
```
Good luck will rub off when I shakes 'ands with you.
```
|Dm        |Am       |E7            |Am          ‖
```

Verse 2

```
Am          |Am(maj7) |Am7        |D
```
I choose me bristles with pride, yes I do.
```
 |Dm        |Am       |B7        |E7
```
A broom for the shaft, and a brush for the flue.
```
|Am        |Am(maj7) |Am7        |D          |
```
```
|Dm        |Am           |E7        |Am          ‖
```

Verse 3

```
Am          |Am(maj7) |Am7        |D
```
Up where the smoke is all billowed and curled,
```
     |Dm        |Am       |B7          |E7
```
'Tween pavement and stars is the chimney sweep world.
```
   |Am            |Am(maj7) |Am        |D
```
When there's hardly no day   an' 'ardly no night,
```
   |Dm        |Am       |E7            |Am
```
There's things half in shadow an' 'alfway in white.
```
   |Dm        |Am           |E7          |Am          ‖
```
On the rooftops of London,   ooh, what a sight!

Chorus 4

```
Am              |Am(maj7)  |Am7            |D
```
Chim chiminey, chim chiminey, chim chim cher - ee!
```
    |Dm        |Am           |B7          |E7          |
```
When you're with a sweep, you're in glad compa - ny.
```
Am        |Am(maj7) |Am7   |D
```
Nowhere is there a more 'appier crew
```
   |Dm        |Am           |E7            |Am          |
```
Than them what sings, "Chim chim cher - ee, chim cher - oo."
```
Dm        |Am           |E7          |Am          ‖
```
Chim chiminey, chim chim cher - ee, chim cher - oo.

Circle of Life
from THE LION KING

Music by Elton John
Lyrics by Tim Rice

(Capo 3rd fret)

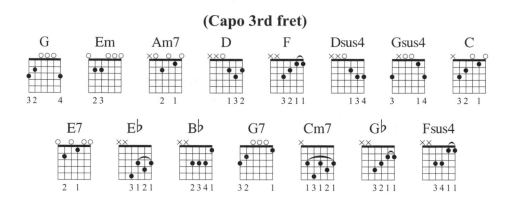

G   Em   Am7   D   F   Dsus4   Gsus4   C

E7   Eb   Bb   G7   Cm7   Gb   Fsus4

Intro

|G |Em |Am7 |D |
|G |Em |Am7 |D

Verse 1

‖G |Am7
From the day we arrive on the plan - et
|D |G
And blinking, step into the sun,
|Em |Am7
There's more to see than can ever be seen;
|F |Dsus4 D   ‖
More to do than can ever be done.

Verse 2

‖G |Am7
There's far too much to take in here;
|D |G
More to find than can ever be found.
|Em |Am7
But the sun rolling high through the sapphire sky
|F |D
Keeps great and small on the endless round.

© 1994 Wonderland Music Company, Inc.
All Rights Reserved. Used by Permission.

20

Chorus 1

‖ **G**   **Gsus4** | **G**
It's the circle of life,
        | **F** |
And it moves us all.
           | **C** |
Through despair and hope,
      | **Dsus4** | **D**
Through faith and love.
     | **G** | **E7**
Till we find our place
         | **Am7** | **E♭**
On the path un - winding
  | **G** | **Dsus4**
In the circle,
   D | **C** | **G**   ‖
The circle of life.

Flute Solo   *Repeat Verses 1 & 2*

Chorus 2

‖ **G**   **Gsus4** | **G**
It's the circle of life,
        | **F** |
And it moves us all.
           | **C** |
Through despair and hope,
      | **Dsus4** | **D**
Through faith and love.
     | **B♭** | **G7**
Till we find our place
         | **Cm7** | **G♭**
On the path un - winding
  | **B♭** | **Fsus4**
In the circle,
   F | **E♭** | **B♭**   ‖
The circle of life.

Colors of the Wind
from POCAHONTAS

Music by Alan Menken
Lyrics by Stephen Schwartz

(Capo 1st fret)

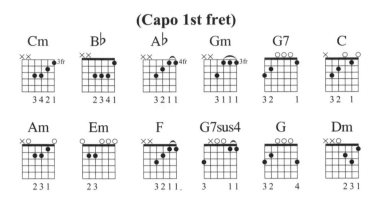

Intro

|Cm |

‖Cm   Bb
You think I'm an ignorant savage,

|Cm
And you've been so many places,

Bb
I guess it must be so.

|Ab   Gm |Ab   Gm
But still I cannot see, if the savage one is me,

|Cm   Ab |G7
How can there be so much that you don't know?

N.C. |C |Am |C |Am
You don't know…

Verse 1

‖C |Am
You think you own whatever land you land on.

|C |Em
The earth is just a dead thing you can claim.

|Am |F
But I know ev'ry rock and tree and creature

|G7sus4 |Am
Has a life, has a spirit, has a name.

Verse 2

```
      ‖C                          |Am
You think the only people who are people
      |C                          |Em
Are the people who look and think like you,
      |Am                         |F
But if you walk in the footsteps of a stranger
         |G7sus4                        |C
You'll learn things you never knew you never knew.
```

Chorus 1

```
         ‖Am                      |Em       F
Have you ever heard the wolf cry to the blue corn moon,
   |Am                      |Em
Or asked the grinning bobcat why he grinned?
      |F           G         |C        Am
Can you sing with all the voices of the mountain?
      |F                         |G7sus4
Can you paint with all the colors of the wind?
      |F              G7sus4    |C    |Am  |C     |Am
Can you paint with all the colors of the wind?
```

Verse 3

```
      ‖C                          |Am
Come run the hidden pine trails of the forest,
      |C                          |Em
Come taste the sun-sweet berries of the earth.
      |Am                      |F
Come roll in all the riches all a - round you,
         |G7sus4                     |Am
And for once never wonder what they're worth.
```

Verse 4

     ‖**C** |**Am**
The rainstorm and the river are my brothers.

     |**C** |**Em**
The heron and the otter are my friends.

     |**Am** |**F**
And we are all connected to each other

     |**Dm**   **G7sus4** |**C**   ‖
In a circle, in a hoop that never ends.

Bridge

Em **F** |**C**   **Am**
How high does the sycamore grow?

    |**B♭** |**F**   **G** |**F**
If you cut it down, then you'll never know.

Chorus 2

G   ‖**Am** |**Em**   **F**
And you'll never hear the wolf cry to the blue corn moon,

    |**Am** |**Em**
For whether we are white or copper-skinned,

       |**F**   **G** |**C**   **Am**
We need to sing with all the voices of the mountain,

     |**F** |**G**
Need to paint with all the colors of the wind.

     |**Dm**   **G** |**Em**
You can own the earth and still all you'll own is earth

    F |**Am**   **F** |**C** |**Am** |
Un - til you can paint with all the colors of the wind.

|**F** |**G** |**C** | ‖

A Dream Is a Wish Your Heart Makes

from CINDERELLA

Words and Music by Mack David,
Al Hoffman and Jerry Livingston

(Capo 3rd fret)

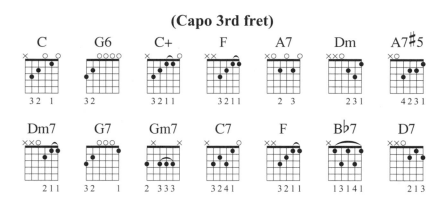

Verse 1

  |**C**   **G6** |**C** |
A dream is a wish your heart makes

        C+ |**F**   **A7**
When you're fast a - sleep.

  |**Dm**   **A7♯5** |**Dm7**
In dreams you will lose your heartaches,

    |**G7** |**C**   **C+** **Dm7** **G7**
What - ever you wish for, you keep.

    |**C** |**G6** |**C**
Have faith in your dreams and someday

   |**Gm7**   **C7** |**F**
Your rainbow will come smiling through.

     |**Dm**   **B♭7**
No matter how your heart is grieving,

    |**C**   **D7**
If you keep on be - lieving,

   |**Dm7**   **G7** |**C**   ‖
The dream that you wish will come true.

Go the Distance

from HERCULES

Music by Alan Menken
Lyrics by David Zippel

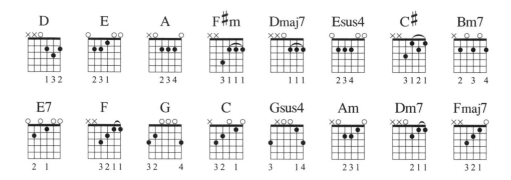

Verse 1

```
      ‖D  E  A          |D  E  A
```
I have of - ten dreamed of a far off place
```
          |D  E  F#m            |Dmaj7  Esus4  E
```
Where a great warm welcome will be waiting for me.
```
          |D    E   A             |D  E  F#m
```
Where the crowds will cheer when they see my face,
```
          |D  C#  F#m          |Dmaj7         Esus4  E
```
And a voice keeps saying this is where I'm meant to be.

Chorus 1

```
      ‖A      Bm7  |
```
I will find my way.
```
A             E
```
I can go the dis - tance.
```
      |A        |Bm7
```
I'll be there some - day
```
A       E    E7
```
If I can be strong.
```
      |A    D       |F#m     |Bm7
```
I know ev'ry mile will be worth my while.
```
      |D  E  A
```
I would go most anywhere
```
      |Dmaj7  Esus4  E     |A          ‖
```
To feel like I _____ be - long.

Interlude |**F**   **G**   **F**   **G**

                                ‖**C**   **F** |
Outro   I am on my way.

                                Gsus4   **G**
                                I can go the dis - tance.

                                    |**C**   **F** |
                                I don't care how far,

                                Gsus4   **G**
                                Somehow I'll be strong.

                                    |**C**   **F** |**Am** |**Dm7**
                                I know ev'ry mile ___ will be worth my while.

                                    |**F** **G**   **C**
                                I would go most anywhere

                                  |**Fmaj7**   **Gsus4** |**C** | ‖
                                To find where I be - long.

God Help the Outcasts

from THE HUNCHBACK OF NOTRE DAME

Music by Alan Menken
Lyrics by Stephen Schwartz

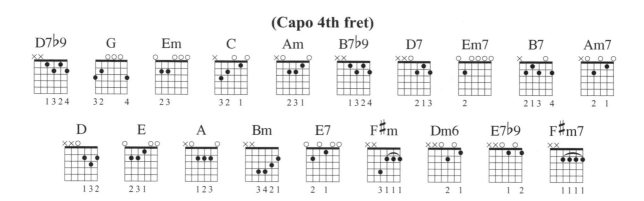

(Capo 4th fret)

Verse 1

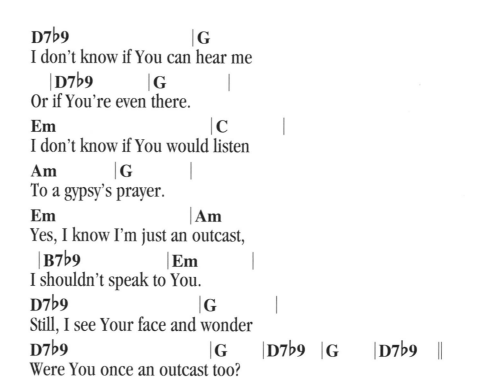

D7♭9 |G
I don't know if You can hear me
 |D7♭9 |G |
Or if You're even there.
Em |C |
I don't know if You would listen
Am |G |
To a gypsy's prayer.
Em |Am
Yes, I know I'm just an outcast,
 |B7♭9 |Em |
I shouldn't speak to You.
D7♭9 |G |
Still, I see Your face and wonder
D7♭9 |G |D7♭9 |G |D7♭9 ‖
Were You once an outcast too?

Chorus 1

G | |C | |
God help the outcasts, hungry from birth.
Am |D7 |G | |
Show them the mercy they don't find on earth.
Em | |Am | |
God help my people, we look to You still.
D7♭9 |G |D7♭9 |G   ‖
God help the outcasts or nobody will.

Verse 2

D7♭9 |G |D7♭9 |Em |Em7
  I ask for wealth.   I ask for fame.
       |C |D7 |G |B7
I ask for glory to shine on my name.
       |Em |Em7 |C |Em
I ask for love   I can pos - sess.
       |Am |Am7 |D |E   ‖
I ask for God and His angels to bless me.

Chorus 2

A | |Bm |
I ask for nothing. I can get by,
  |E7 | |A | |
But I know so many less lucky than I.
F♯m | |Bm | |
Please help my people, the poor and down - trod.
Dm6 |A |E7♭9 |F♯m | |
I thought we all were the children of God.
E7♭9 |A   F♯m |E7♭9 |A   ‖
God help the out - casts, children of God.

Outro

E7♭9 |A |E7♭9 |F♯m |
F♯m7 |D |E |A   ‖

He's a Tramp
from LADY AND THE TRAMP

Words and Music by
Peggy Lee and Sonny Burke

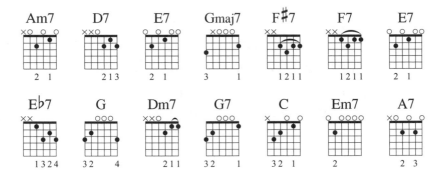

Verse 1

```
       ‖Am7  D7         |Am7        D7
He's a tramp,    but they love him.
           |Am7    E7      |Am7        D7
Breaks a new heart    ev'ry - day.
         |Gmaj7 F#7        |F7        E7
He's a tramp,        they a - dore him
           |Eb7           D7    |G      E7
And I only hope he'll stay that way.
```

Verse 2

```
       ‖Am7  D7         |Am7        D7
He's a tramp,    he's a scoundrel,
          |Am7    E7      |Am7        D7
He's a rounder,    he's a cad,
         |Gmaj7 F#7        |F7        E7
He's a tramp,        but I love him.
         |Eb7          D7        |G
Yes, even I have got it pretty bad.
```

Bridge

‖**Dm7 G7** |**Dm7** **G7** |**C**
You can never tell when he'll show up.

G7 |**C** |**Em7**
He gives you plenty of trouble.

A7 |**Em7** **A7** |**Am7**
I guess he's just a no 'count pup.

E7 |**Am7 D7**
But I wish that he were double.

Verse 3

‖**Am7 D7** |**Am7** **D7**
He's a tramp,   he's a rover

|**Am7 E7** |**Am7 D7**
And there's nothing more to say.

|**Gmaj7 F♯7** |**F7** **E7**
If he's a tramp,   he's a good one

|**E♭7** **D7** |**G** **E7**
And I wish that I could travel his way.

E♭7 **D7** |**G** **E7**
Wish that I could travel his way,

E♭7 **D7** |**G** ‖
Wish that I could travel his way.

Heigh-Ho

**The Dwarfs' Marching Song from
SNOW WHITE AND THE SEVEN DWARFS**

Words by Larry Morey
Music by Frank Churchill

(Capo 3rd fret)

G   C   A7   D7

Verse 1

‖**G** |**C**
"Heigh-ho, heigh-ho,"

 |**A7** |**D7**
To make your troubles go,

 |**C**   **G** |**C**
Just keep on singing all day long,

 |**G** |**D7**
"Heigh-ho, heigh-ho, heigh-ho.

 |**G** |**C**
Heigh-ho, heigh-ho,"

 |**A7** |**D7**
For if you're feeling low,

 |**C**   **G** |**C**
You posi - tively can't go wrong

 |**G**   **D7** |**G**
With a "Heigh,   heigh-ho."

Verse 2

‖**G** |**C**
"Heigh-ho, heigh-ho,"

 |**A7** |**D7**
It's home from work we go,

 |**C**   **G** |**C**
Whistle melody...

 |**G** |**D7**
"Heigh-ho, heigh-ho, heigh-ho.

 |**G** |**C**
Heigh-ho, heigh-ho,"

 |**A7** |**D7**
All seven in a row,

 |**C**   **G** |**C**
Whistle melody...

 |**G**   **D7** |**G**   ‖
With a "Heigh,   heigh-ho."

I See the Light

from TANGLED

Music by Alan Menken
Lyrics by Glenn Slater

(Capo 3rd fret)

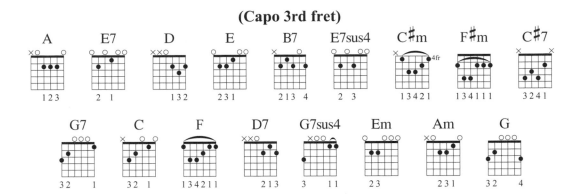

Intro

|A | | | ||

Verse 1

A |E7   A |
All those days, watching from the windows.

     |E7   A |
All those years, outside, looking in.

D |A   D   E |
All that time, never even know - ing

A   B7 |E7sus4   E7 |
Just how blind I've been.

A |E7   A |
Now I'm here, blinking in the starlight.

     |E7   A |
Now I'm here, suddenly I see.

D |C#m
Standing here, it's, oh, so clear

     |F#m   B7 |E7sus4   E7
I'm where I'm meant to be.

Chorus 1

```
         ‖D          |A
And at last I see the light,
         |E7              |A
And it's like the fog has lifted.
         |D          |A
And at last I see the light,
         |C♯7         |F♯m
And it's like the sky is new.
         |D              |A
And it's warm and real and bright,
         |C♯m             |D       |          |
And the world has somehow shifted.
A        |E7          A       |
All at once, ev'rything looks diff'rent,
D        E7   |A       |          |        |        ‖
Now that I  see  you.
```

Oboe Solo

```
            |A          |E7   A   |           |E7      A      |
            |D          |A    D  E |A    B7   |E7sus4  E7     |G7         ‖
```

Verse 2

```
C              |G7          C            |
All these days, chasing down a daydream.
               |G7      C           |
All those years living in a blur.
F          |C       F    G7   |
All that time, never truly see - ing
C      D7           |G7sus4  G7    |
Things    the way they were.
C              |G7          C            |
Now, she's here, shining in the starlight.
               |G7      C         |
Now she's here, suddenly I know.
F                |Em
If she's here, it's crystal clear
   |Am        D7    |G7sus4     G7
I'm where I'm meant to go.
```

Chorus 2

```
        ‖F          |C
And at last I see the light,
        |G7              |C
And it's like the fog has lifted.
        |F              |C
And at last I see the light,
        |E7              |Am
And it's like the sky is new.
        |F                  |C
And it's warm and real and bright,
        |Em                 |G    F    |
And the world has somehow shift - ed.
C          |G7      C          |
All at once, ev'ryting is diff'rent,
F      G7 |C          |Am  D7    |
Now that I see you,
G7sus4  |G7  |C        |        |        ‖
Now  that  I  see you.
```

How Far I'll Go
from MOANA

Music and Lyrics by Lin-Manuel Miranda

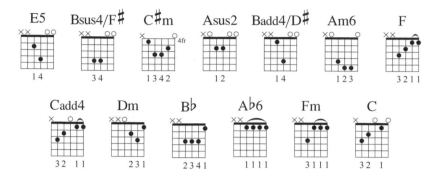

Verse 1

    E5   **|Bsus4/F♯**   **|C♯m**
I've been staring at the edge of the water long as I can re - member,

               |Asus2   **|**
Never really know - ing why.

    E5   **|Bsus4/F♯**   **|C♯m**
I wish I could be the perfect daughter, but I come back to the water,

               |Asus2
No matter how hard I try.

    |C♯m
Ev'ry turn I take, ev'ry trail I track,

     |Badd4/D♯
Ev'ry path I make, ev'ry road leads back

     |E5
To the place I know where I cannot go,

      |Am6   **|**
Where I long to be.

Chorus 1

       ‖E5
See the line where the sky meets the sea?

     |Bsus4/F♯
It calls ____ me.

      |C♯m   **|Asus2**
And no one knows how far it goes.

     |E5   **|Bsus4/F♯**
If the wind in my sail on the sea stays behind ____ me,

     |C♯m
One day I'll know.

     |Am6   **‖**
If I go, there's just no telling how far I'll go.

Verse 2

```
E5                           |Bsus4/F♯                    |C♯m
```
I know ev'rybody on this island seems so happy on this island.
```
                      |Asus2        |
```
Ev'rything is by de - sign.
```
E5                           |Bsus4/F♯            |C♯m
```
I know ev'rybody on this island has a role on this island,
```
                      |Asus2
```
So maybe I can roll with ____ mine.
```
     |C♯m
```
I can lead with pride, I can make us strong,
```
        |Bsus4/D♯
```
I'll be satisfied if I play along.
```
          |E5
```
But the voice inside sings a diff'rent song.
```
        |Am6             |
```
What is wrong with me?

Chorus 2

```
              ‖E5                            |Bsus4/F♯
```
See the light as it shines on the sea? It's blind - ing.
```
          |C♯m             |Asus2
```
But no one knows how deep it goes.
```
          |E5
```
And it seems like it's calling out to me,
```
              |Bsus4/F♯        |C♯m
```
So come find ____ me and let me know.
```
          |Am6
```
What's be - yond that line? Will I cross that line?

Chorus 3

```
              ‖F
```
See the line where the sky meets the sea?
```
          |Cadd4
```
It calls ____ me.
```
            |Dm              |B♭
```
And no one knows how far it goes.
```
     |F                                  |Cadd4
```
If the wind in my sail on the sea stays behind ____ me,
```
            |Dm            |A♭6    Fm  B♭  |C              ‖
```
One day I'll know how far I'll go.

I Wan'na Be Like You
(The Monkey Song)
from THE JUNGLE BOOK

Words and Music by
Richard M. Sherman and Robert B. Sherman

(Capo 3rd fret)

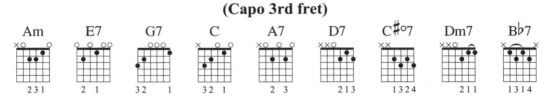

| Am | E7 | G7 | C | A7 | D7 | C#°7 | Dm7 | B♭7 |

Verse 1

‖**Am** |
Now I'm the king of the swingers,
        | |**E7**
The jungle V.I.P.
        | |
I've reached the top and had to stop,
        | |**Am**
And that's what's botherin' me.
        | |
I wanna be a man, man-cub,
        | |**E7**
And stroll right into town,
        | |
And be just like the other men,
        | |**Am**
I'm tired of monkeyin' 'round!

Chorus 1

G7 ‖**C** |
Oh,   ooh, ooh, ooh! (Ee - ee.)
                    |**A7** |
I wanna be like you, ooh, ooh! (Ee - ee.)
          |**D7** |**G7** |
I wanna walk like you, talk like you,
C   **C#°7** |**Dm7**
Too, ooh, ooh, (Ee - ee.)
        G7 |**C** |
You'll see it's true, ooh, ooh! (Ee - ee.)
          |**A7** |
An ape like me, ee, ee (ooh, ooh,)
        |**D7** |**G7**
Can learn to be hu-ooh-ooh-man,
C |**D7** **E7**
Too, ooh, ooh. (Ee - ee.)

Verse 2

```
 ‖Am              |
Don't try to kid me, man-cub,
                    |E7
I made a deal with you.
        |          |
What I desire is man's red fire,
   |                    |Am
To make my dream come true!
   |          |
Give me the secret, man-cub,
        |          |E7
C'mon clue me what to do.
   |          |
Give me the pow'r of man's red flow'r,
   |          |Am
So I can be like you.
```

Chorus 2

```
G7 ‖C                    |
Oh,   ooh, ooh, ooh! (Ee - ee.)
             |A7              |
I wanna be like you, ooh, ooh! (Ee - ee.)
        |D7        |G7          |
I wanna walk like you, talk like you,
C          C♯°7    |Dm7
Too, ooh, ooh, (Ee - ee.)
       G7    |C              |
You'll see it's true, ooh, ooh! (Ee - ee.)
             |A7              |
Someone like me, ee, ee (ooh, ooh,)
   |D7        |G7              |C   B♭7  |A7
Can learn to be like someone like me,
      |D7        |G7              |C   B♭7  |A7
Can learn to be like someone like you,
      |D7        |G7              |C      |        ‖
Can learn to be like someone like me.
```

I Won't Say (I'm in Love)

from HERCULES

Music by Alan Menken
Lyrics by David Zippel

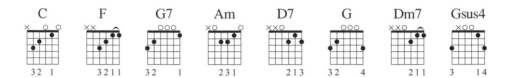

Verse 1

C |F |C
If there's a prize rotten judgment,

|F   G7 |
I guess I've already won that.

Am |D7 |G
No man is worth the aggra - vation.

|F   G7   F   G   ‖
That's ancient history, been there, done that.

Pre-Chorus 1

C |F   G |
Who d'ya think you're kiddin', he's the earth and heaven to you.

C |Am |
Try to keep it hidden, honey, we can see right through you.

F |C
Girl, ya can't conceal it, we know how ya feel

|Dm7 |Gsus4   G
And who you're thinking of.

Chorus 1

‖C | |Am
Oh. ____ No chance, no way, I won't say it, no, no.

| |F
You swoon, you sigh, why deny it uh, oh.

Gsus4 | G |C | G7 ‖
It's too cli - ché,   I won't say I'm in love.

Verse 2

```
          C                                    |F      |C
              I thought my heart and learned its lesson.
                                       |G7      |Am
          It feels so good when you start ____ out.
                                   |D7          |G
          My head is screaming, get a grip,  girl,
                                   |F  G7  F    G    ||
          Unless you're dying to cry your heart out.
```

Pre-Chorus 2

```
          C                       |F          G               |
              You keep on denying who you are and how you're feeling.
          C                   |Am                        |
          Baby, we're not buying, hon, we saw ya hit the ceiling.
          F                   |C
          Face it like a grown-up, when ya gonna own up
              |Dm7           |Gsus4  G     |
          That ya got, got, got it bad?
```

Chorus 2

```
              ||C                |                 |Am
          Woh. ____ No chance, no way, I won't say it, no, no.
                        |                        |F
          Give up, give in. Check the grin, you're in love.
                            |                |G
          This scene won't play, I won't say I'm in love.
                            |                        |C
          You're doin' flips, read our lips, you're in love.
                            |                |Am
          You're way off base. I won't say it.
                        |              |F
          Get off my case, I won't say it.
                  |Gsus4              G    |C          |
          Girl, don't be proud, it's O.K. you're in love.
          Am  |F               Gsus4  |                    |
          Oh. _____ At least out loud,
                  G     |C      |       |       |       ||
          I won't say I'm in love.
```

I'll Make a Man out of You

from MULAN

Music by Matthew Wilder
Lyrics by David Zippel

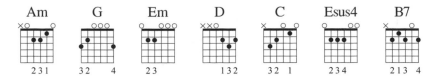

Intro |Am | G ||

Verse 1

        Em   **D**   **G** |
Let's get down to bus - 'ness

           |**Am**   **D** | |
To de - feat the Huns.

Em   **D**   **G** |
Did they send me daugh - ters

           |**Am**   **D** |
When I asked for sons?

            |**C** |**D**
You're the saddest bunch I ever met.

           |**G** |**C** |
But you can bet before we're through,

        | **D** | |**Em**   **D** |**Em** ||
Mister, I'll make a man out of you.

Verse 2

```
Em      D   G   |
```
Tranquil as a for - est,

```
        |Am      |D        |
```
But on fire with - in.

```
Em      D       G   |
```
Once you find your cen - ter,

```
        |Am   D      |
```
You are sure to win.

```
         |C              D  |
```
You're a spineless, pale, pa - thetic lot

```
         |G          C  |
```
And you haven't got a clue.

```
                |       D  |      Em   |  D  Esus4 |            ||
```
Somehow I'll make a man out of you.

Bridge

```
C                      D              |
```
   I'm never gonna catch my breath.

```
B7                             Em        |
```
Say goodbye to those who knew ___ me.

```
D            G               |C         |
```
Boy, was I a fool in school for cutting gym.

```
                        D             |
```
This guy's got 'em scared to death.

```
B7                    Em          |
```
Hope he doesn't see right through me.

```
D              G            |C
```
Now I really wish that I ___ knew how to swim.

Chorus 1

```
      D  C    ||                D            |        G     |C
```
Be a man! ___ We must be swift as the cours - ing riv - er,

```
                                              Be a man!
```

```
        D            |B7     Em         |C
```
With all the force of a great ___ typhoon,

```
                             Be a man!
```

```
        D            |B7  Em
```
With all the strength of a rag - ing fire,

```
   |C              |D           |   Em|          ||
```
Mys - terious as the dark ___ side of the moon.
```
```

Verse 3

Em   D   G |
Time is racing toward us

    |Am |D |
'Till the Huns ar - rive.

Em   D G |
Heed my ev'ry or - der

    |Am   D |
And you might sur - vive.

     |C   D |
You're un - suited for the rage of war.

    |G   C |
So pack up, go home, you're through.

    | D | Em |D Esus4
How could I make a man out of you?

Chorus 2

C D C   ‖   D | G |C
Be a man! ___ We must be swift as the cours - ing riv - er,

                            Be a man!

        D |B7   Em |C
With all the force of a great ___ ty - phoon,

                   Be a man!

        D |B7 Em
With all the strength of a rag - ing fire,

    |C |D   Em | D Em |
Mys - terious as the dark ___ side of the moon.

C D C | N.C. | |
Be a man! ___ We must be swift as the cours - ing river,

                           Be a man!

                | |
With all the force of a great ___ typhoon,

                   Be a man!

                |
With all the strength of a rag - ing fire,

    |C   D | | Em ‖
Mys - terious as the dark side of the moon.

Kiss the Girl
from THE LITTLE MERMAID

Music by Alan Menken
Lyrics by Howard Ashman

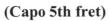
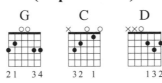

(Capo 5th fret)

Verse 1

G

   There you see her,

Sitting there across the way.

C |G

She don't got a lot to say, but there's something a - bout her.

    |D |C

And you don't   know why, but you're   dying to try.

    |G

You wanna   kiss the girl.

Verse 2

G

   Yes, you want her.

Look at her; you know you do.

C |G

Possible she wants you, too.   There's one way to ask her.

    |D |C

It don't take a word, not a single word.

    |G

Go on and   kiss the girl.

Chorus 1

G |C
Sha la la la la la, my, oh, my.
        |G
Look at the boy, too shy.
          |D |G
Ain't gonna   kiss the girl.
          |C
Sha la la la la la, ain't that sad.
      |D
Ain't it a shame, too bad.
      |G | ‖
He gonna miss the girl.

Verse 3

G | |
Now's your mo - ment,

              | |
Floating in a blue lagoon.
C |
Boy, you better do it soon;
        |G |
Time will be better.
        |D |C
She don't say a word and she won't   say a word
        |G | ‖
Until you kiss the girl.

Chorus 2

G |C
 Sha la la la la la, don't be scared.

  |G
You got the mood prepared;

  |D |G
Go on and kiss the girl.

       |C
Sha la la la la la, don't stop now.

  |D
Don't try to hide it how

  |G   ‖
You wanna kiss the girl.

Outro-Chorus

G |C
 Sha la la la la la, float along

  |G
And listen to the song;

    |D |G
The song says, "Kiss the girl."

    |C
Sha la la la la la, music play.

   |D
Do what the music say.

   |G | |
You gotta kiss the girl.

    | |
Kiss the girl.

    | |
Kiss the girl.

    |
Kiss the girl.

   | | | ‖
Go on and kiss the girl.

Lava
from LAVA

Music and Lyrics by
James Ford Murphy

C   G7   F

3 2 1   3 2   1   3 2 1 1

Intro

|C | |G7 | |

|F | |C |G7 | ||

Verse 1

C | |G7 | |F
   A long, long time ago   there was a volcano
     | |C |G7 | |
Living all alone in the middle of the sea.
C | |G7 | |F
He sat high a - bove his bay, watching all the couples play,
   | |C |G7 | |C
And wishing that he had someone too.
   | |G7 |
And from his lava came this song of hope
     |F | |C |G7 | ||
That he sang out loud ev'ry day for years and years.

Chorus 1

F | |C |
   "I have a dream ____ I hope will come true,
  |G7 | |C |
That you're here with me, and I'm here with you.
 |F | |C |
I wish that the earth, sea, and the sky up a - bove-a
 |F |G7 |C | ||
Will send me someone to lava."

Interlude 1

|F | |G7 | |

| |C | | ||

Verse 2

C | |G7 |
Years of singing all alone turned his lava into stone,
|F | |C |G7 | |C
Un - til   he was on the brink of extinct - tion.
| |G7 |
But little did he know that, living in the sea below,
|F | |C |G7 | |C
An - other volcano was listening to his song.
| |G7 |
Ev'ry day she heard his tune, her lava grew and grew,
|F | |C |G7 | |C
Be - cause she believed his song was meant for her.
| |G7 |
Now she was so ready to meet him a - bove the sea,
|F | |C |G7 | ||
As he sang his song of hope for the last time.

Chorus 2   *Repeat Chorus 1*

Interlude 2 |C | ||

Verse 3

C | |G7 | |F
Rising from the sea below stood a lovely volcano,
| |C |G7 |
Looking all around, but she could not see him.
|C | |G7 |
He tried to sing to let her know that she was not there alone,
|F | |C |G7 |
But with no lava his song was all gone.
|C |
He filled the sea with his tears,
|G7 |
And watched his dreams disappear
|F | |C |G7 | ||
As she re - membered what his song meant to her.

Chorus 3   *Repeat Chorus 1*

Interlude 3 |C | | | ‖

Verse 4

C | |G7 | |F
Oh, they were so happy to fin'lly meet a - bove the sea.
            | |C |G7 |
All to - gether now their lava grew and grew.
    |C |
No longer are they all alone
        |G7 | |F
With a - loha as their new home,
            | |C |G7 | ‖
And when you visit them this is what they sing.

Outro-Chorus

F | |C |
    "I have a dream ___ I hope will come true,
    |G7 | |C | |
That you'll grow old with me ___ and I'll grow old with you.
F | |C | |
We thank the earth, sea, and the sky we thank too,
    F |G7 |C | |
"I   lava   you."
    F |G7 |C | |
"I   lava   you."
    F |G7 |C | ‖
"I   lava   you."

Let It Go

from FROZEN

Music and Lyrics by
Kristen Anderson-Lopez and Robert Lopez

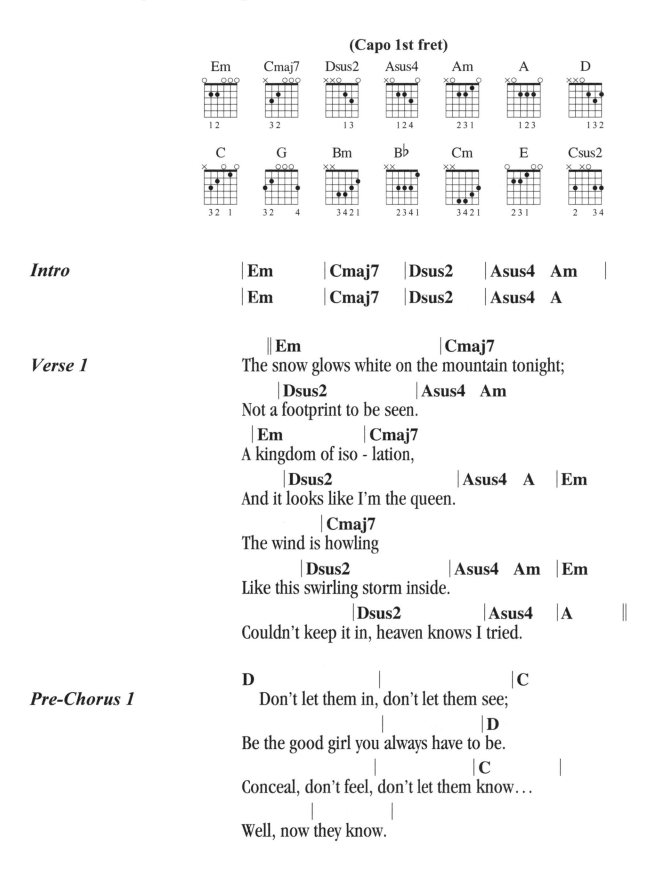

(Capo 1st fret)

Intro

| Em | | Cmaj7 | Dsus2 | Asus4 Am | |
| Em | | Cmaj7 | Dsus2 | Asus4 A |

Verse 1

‖ **Em** |**Cmaj7**
The snow glows white on the mountain tonight;

|**Dsus2** |**Asus4   Am**
Not a footprint to be seen.

|**Em** |**Cmaj7**
A kingdom of iso - lation,

|**Dsus2** |**Asus4   A** |**Em**
And it looks like I'm the queen.

|**Cmaj7**
The wind is howling

|**Dsus2** |**Asus4   Am** |**Em**
Like this swirling storm inside.

|**Dsus2** |**Asus4** |**A**   ‖
Couldn't keep it in, heaven knows I tried.

Pre-Chorus 1

D | |**C**
  Don't let them in, don't let them see;

| |**D**
Be the good girl you always have to be.

| |**C** |
Conceal, don't feel, don't let them know…

| |
Well, now they know.

Chorus 1

N.C. ‖ **G** | **D**
Let it go, let it go,
  | **Em** | **C**
Can't hold it back any - more.
  | **G** | **D**
Let it go, let it go,
   | **Em** | **C** |
Turn a - way and slam the door.
G | **D** | **Em** | **C**
I don't care what they're going to say.
  | **Bm** | **B**♭
Let the storm rage on,
  | **C** | | **G** | **D**   ‖
The cold never bothered me an - yway.

Verse 2

Em | **C**
  It's funny how some dis - tance
   | **D** | **Am**
Makes ev'rything seem small,
   | **Em** | **D**
And the fears that once controlled me
   | **Asus4** | **A**   ‖
Can't get to me at all.

Pre-Chorus 2

D | | **C**
  It's time to see what I can do,
          | | **D**
To test the lim - its and break through.
        | | **C**
No right, no wrong, no rules for me,
  | |
I'm free!

Chorus 2

```
N.C. ‖ G        | D
Let it go, let it go,
       | Em                    | C
I am one with the wind and sky.
       | G        | D
Let it go, let it go,
       | Em            | C           |
You'll never see me cry.
G      D       |     | Em      C     |
Here I stand,    and here I'll stay,
       | Bm          Bb |             ‖
Let the storm rage on.
```

Interlude

```
| C              |              |              |              ‖
```

Bridge

```
C              |                    |                    |                    |
    My power flurries through the air into the ground.
         |              |              |              | D
My soul is spiraling in frozen fractals all around.
              |              |              | E
And one thought crystallizes like an icy blast;
         | C              | D          | Am          | C
I'm never going back. The past is in the past!
```

Chorus 3

```
N.C. ‖ G        | D
Let it go, let it go,
       | Em                    | C
And I'll rise like the break of dawn.
       | G        | D
Let it go, let it go,
       | Em            | C           |
That perfect girl is gone.
G      D       |     | Em      C     |          | Cm
Here I stand    in the light of day,
       | Bm          Bb |            |
Let the storm rage on.
       | Csus2                |        |        ‖
The cold never bothered me an - yway.
```

Mickey Mouse March
from THE MICKEY MOUSE CLUB

Words and Music by
Jimmie Dodd

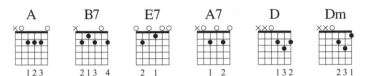

Verse 1

A
Who's the leader of the club
|B7 |E7 |
That's made for you and me?
A   A7 |D   Dm |
M - I - C - K - E - Y
A   E7 |A   ‖
M - O - U - S - E!

Verse 2

A
Hey, there! Hi, there! Ho, there!
     |B7 |E7 |
You're as welcome as can be!
A   A7 |D   Dm |
M - I - C - K - E - Y
A   E7 |A
M - O - U - S - E!

Bridge

     ‖D |
Mickey Mouse! (Donald Duck!)
     |A |
Mickey Mouse! (Donald Duck!)
     |B7 | |E7
For - ever let us hold our banner high!
          | ‖
(High! High! High!)

Verse 3

A |
Come along and sing a song
     |B7 |E7 |
And join the jambo - ree!
A   A7 |D   Dm |
M - I - C - K - E - Y
A   E7 |A   ‖
M - O - U - S - E!

Once Upon a Dream

from SLEEPING BEAUTY

Words and Music by Sammy Fain and Jack Lawrence
Adapted from a theme by Tchaikovsky

(Capo 5th fret)

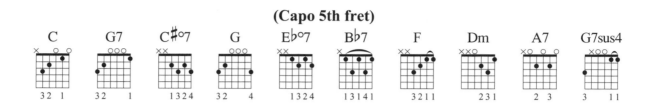

Verse

C | |
I know you!

| |**G7** |**C#°7** |**G7** | |
I walked with you once up - on a dream.

G |**Eb°7** |**Bb7**
I know you!

|**G7** |**C**
The gleam in your eyes

|**F C** |**G7** |
Is so fa - miliar a gleam.

|**C** | |
Yet, I know it's true

| |**Dm** |**A7** |**Dm** |
That visions are seldom all they seem.

Eb°7 |**C** |**A7**
But if I know you,

|**Dm** |**Eb°7**
I know what you'll do;

|**C** |**C#°7** |**A7** |
You'll love me at once the way you did

Dm |**G7sus4 G7** |**C** | ||
Once up - on a dream.

Part of Your World
from THE LITTLE MERMAID

Music by Alan Menken
Lyrics by Howard Ashman

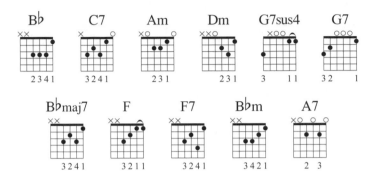

Verse

B♭ |**C7** |
Look at this stuff. Isn't it neat?

B♭ |**C7** |
Wouldn't you think my col - lection's complete?

Am |**Dm**
Wouldn't you think I'm the girl,

     |**G7sus4** |**G7** |
The girl who has ev'rything.

B♭ |**C7** |
Look at this trove, treasures untold.

B♭ |**C7** |
How many wonders can one cavern hold?

Am |**Dm**
Looking around here you'd think

     |**G7sus4** |**G7**
Sure, she's got ev'rything.

Pre-Chorus

```
           ‖ B♭maj7              | Am
I've got gadgets and gizmos a - plenty.
           | Dm                  | G7sus4   G7
I've got who-zits and what-zits ga - lore.
           | B♭maj7              | Am
You want thing-a-ma-bobs, I've got twenty.
           | Dm         |        G7sus4   G7
But who cares? No big deal.
           | C7         |                 ‖
I want more.
```

Chorus 1

```
F                        | Am              |
I wanna be where the people are.
B♭                       | C7              |
I wanna see, wanna see 'em dancin',
Dm                       | Am              | C7              |
Walkin' around on those, what-d'-ya call 'em, oh feet.
F                        | Am              |
Flippin' your fins you don't get too far.
B♭                       | C7              |
Legs are required for jumpin', dancin'.
Dm                       | Am              | C7
Strollin' along down the,    what's the word again,    street.
           | F              | F7
Up where they walk, up where they run,
           | B♭             | B♭m
Up where they stay all day in the sun.
           | F              | C7           | F
Wanderin' free, wish I could be part of that world.
```

Bridge

```
        ‖Bb          |C7           |Am       |Dm
What would I give if I could live outta these waters.
              |Bb          |C7           |Am       |F7
What would I pay to spend a day warm on the sand?
        |Bb          |C7
Betcha on land they under - stand.
         |A7                 |Dm
Bet they don't reprimand their daugh - ters.
         |G7sus4       |G7
Bright young women, sick of swimmin',
       |C7      |
Ready to stand.
```

Chorus 2

```
        ‖F                      |Am            |
And ready to know what the people know.
Bb                      |C7              |
Ask 'em my questions and get some answers.
Dm              |Am                  |C7      |
What's a fire, and why does it, what's the word,   burn?
            |F
When's it my turn?
       |F7          |Bb              |Bbm     |
Wouldn't I love, love to ex - plore that shore up a - bove,
N.C.        |F
Out of the sea.
          |C7          |Bb    C7 |Bb   C7 |F          ‖
Wish I could be part of that world.
```

Reflection
from MULAN

Music by Matthew Wilder
Lyrics by David Zippel

(Capo 2nd fret)

Verse 1

E |C#m
Look at me, I will never pass

 |F#m | B7 |
For a perfect bride or a perfect daughter.

E |C#m |D7 |
Can it be I'm not meant to play this part?

G |Em7 |Am7 |
Now I see that if I were truly to be myself,

Am7♭5 |G | ||
I would break my fam'ly's heart.

Chorus

G |Em7 |
Who is that girl I see

Cadd#11 C |Cm |
Staring straight back at me?

G Em7 |C |
Why is my re - flection someone

F |D7 |
I don't know?

G |Em7 |Cadd#11 |
Somehow I cannot hide

  C |Cm |
Who I am, though I've tried.

G Em7 |C |
When will my re - flection show

Cm |Em Em7 C#m7♭5|
Who I am in - side?

G Em7 |Am7 |
When will my re - flection show

Cm |G |Em |G | ||
Who I am in - side?

Some Day My Prince Will Come

from SNOW WHITE AND THE SEVEN DWARFS

Words by Larry Morey
Music by Frank Churchill

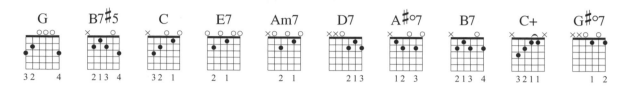

Verse 1

G   **|B7#5** **|C**   **|E7**   **|**
Some - day my prince will come,

Am7 **|**   **|D7**   **|**
Some - day I'll find my love,

    |G   **|A#°7**   **|Am7**   **|D7**   **|**
And how thrilling that moment will be,

    |G   **|A#°7**   **|Am7**   **|D7**   **|**
When the prince of my dreams comes to me.

G **|B7#5** **|C**   **|E7**   **|**
He'll whisper "I love you,"

Am7 **|**   **|D7**   **|**
And   steal a kiss or two.

     |G **|B7**   **|C+**   **|A#°7**
Though he's far a - way, I'll find my love some - day,

   |G   **G#°7** **|Am7** **D7** **|G**   **|Am7** **D7** **||**
Some - day when my   dreams come true.

Verse 2

G   **|B7#5** **|C**   **|E7**   **|**
Some - day I'll find my love,

Am7 **|**   **|D7**   **|**
Some - one to call my own,

    |G   **|A#°7**   **|Am7**   **|D7**   **|**
And I'll know her the moment we meet,

    |G   **|A#°7**   **|Am7**   **|D7**   **|**
For my heart will start skipping a beat.

G **|B7#5** **|C**   **|E7**   **|**
Some - day we'll say and do

Am7 **|**   **|D7**   **|**
Things we've been longing to.

     |G **|B7**   **|C+**   **|A#°7**
Though she's far a - way, I'll find my love some - day,

   |G   **G#°7** **|Am7** **D7** **|G**   **|**   **||**
Some - day when my   dreams come true.

When You Wish upon a Star

from PINOCCHIO

Words by Ned Washington
Music by Leigh Harline

(Capo 4th fret)

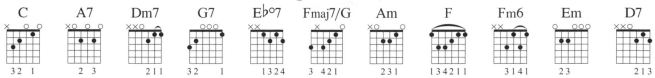

Verse 1

C   A7 |Dm7 |
When you wish up - on a star,

G7 |Eb°7   C |
Makes no diff'rence who you are,

Eb°7 |Dm7   Fmaj7/G
Any - thing your heart de - sires

|Dm7 G7 |C   G7 ||
Will come to   you.

Verse 2

C   A7 |Dm7 |
If your heart is in your dream,

G7 |Eb°7   C |
No request is too ex - treme,

Eb°7 |Dm7 Fmaj7/G
When you wish up - on a star

|Dm7 G7 |C ||
As dream - ers do.

Bridge

Fm6   G7 |C |Fm6
Fate is   kind,

G7 |Eb°7   C |Am
She brings to   those who love,

|Eb°7   D7 |Fm6 |G7 ||
The sweet fulfillment of their secret long - ing.

Verse 3

C   A7 |Dm7 |
Like a bolt out of the blue,

G7 |Eb°7   C |
Fate steps in and sees you thru,

| Eb°7 |Dm7 Fmaj7/G
When you wish up - on a star

|Dm7 G7 |C ||
Your dream comes true.

Supercalifragilisticexpialidocious

from MARY POPPINS

Words and Music by
Richard M. Sherman and Robert B. Sherman

(Capo 3rd fret)

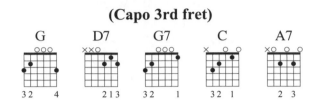

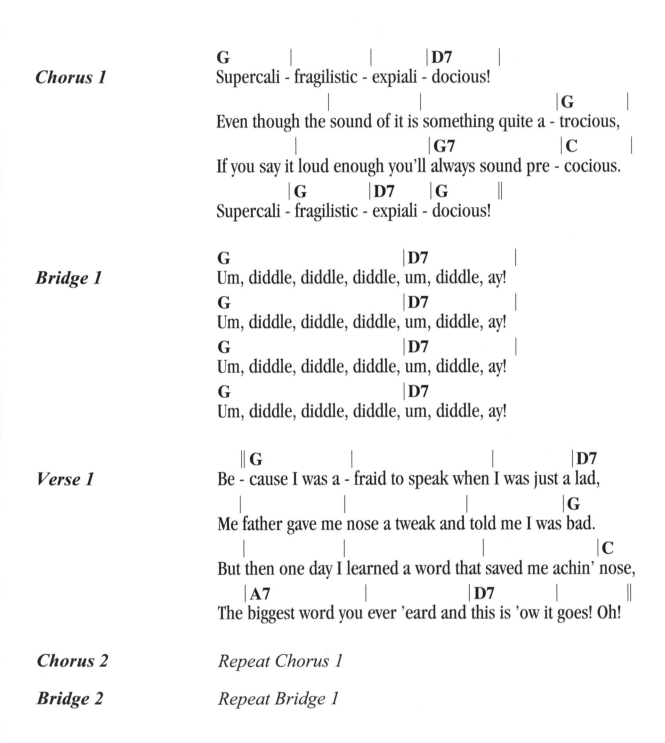

Chorus 1

G | | |**D7** |
Supercali - fragilistic - expiali - docious!

| | |**G** |
Even though the sound of it is something quite a - trocious,

| |**G7** |**C** |
If you say it loud enough you'll always sound pre - cocious.
|**G** |**D7** |**G** ‖
Supercali - fragilistic - expiali - docious!

Bridge 1

G |**D7** |
Um, diddle, diddle, diddle, um, diddle, ay!
G |**D7** |
Um, diddle, diddle, diddle, um, diddle, ay!
G |**D7** |
Um, diddle, diddle, diddle, um, diddle, ay!
G |**D7**
Um, diddle, diddle, diddle, um, diddle, ay!

Verse 1

‖**G** | | |**D7**
Be - cause I was a - fraid to speak when I was just a lad,
| | | |**G**
Me father gave me nose a tweak and told me I was bad.
| | | |**C**
But then one day I learned a word that saved me achin' nose,
|**A7** | |**D7** | ‖
The biggest word you ever 'eard and this is 'ow it goes! Oh!

Chorus 2   *Repeat Chorus 1*

Bridge 2   *Repeat Bridge 1*

Verse 2

‖ G | | |D7
He traveled all a - round the world, and ev'rywhere he went,

| | | |G
He'd use his word and all would say, "There goes a clever gent."

| | | |C
When dukes and maha - rajahs pass the time 'o day with me,

|A7 | | |D7 ‖
I say me special word and then they ask me out to tea! Oh!

Chorus 3   *Repeat Chorus 1*

Bridge 3   *Repeat Bridge 1*

Verse 3

‖ G | | |D7
So when the cat has got your tongue, there's no need for dis - may,

| | | |G
Just summon up this word and then you've got a lot to say.

| | |G7 |C
But better use it carefully or it could change your life.

|A7 | | |D7
One night I said it to my girl and now me girl's me wife!

Chorus 4

‖ G | | |D7 |
She's supercali - fragilistic - expiali - docious!

| | |G |
Supercali - fragilistic - expiali - docious!

| |G7 |C |
Supercali - fragilistic - expiali - docious!

|G |D7 |G ‖
Supercali - fragilistic - expiali - docious!

Outro |C |G |D7 |G ‖

Under the Sea
from THE LITTLE MERMAID

Music by Alan Menken
Lyrics by Howard Ashman

(Capo 3rd fret)

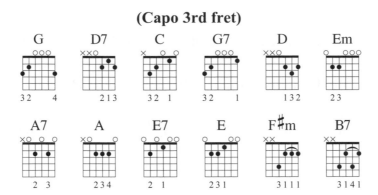

Intro

‖: G |D7   G | |D7   G   :‖

Verse 1

G |D7   G |
    The seaweed is always greener

|D7   G |
In somebody else's lake.

       |D7   G |
You dream about going up there,

     |D7   G |C
But that is a big mis - take.

         |G |D7
Just look at the world around you,

          |G |C
Right here on the ocean floor.

        |G |D7
Such wonderful things surround you.

        |G |
What more is you lookin' for?

Chorus 1

N.C.   ‖C |G |D7 |G
Under the sea,   under the sea.
    |C |D7
Darlin', it's better down where it's wetter,
    |G |G7
Take it from me.
    |C |D
Up on the shore, they work all day.
    |Em |A7
Out in the sun, they slave away
    |C |D7
While we de - votin' full time to floatin'
    |G |D7 G | |D7 G ‖
Under the sea.

Verse 2

G |D7   G |
Down here, all the fish is happy
      |D7   G |
As off through the waves they roll.
   |D7   G |
The fish on the land ain't happy.
     |D7 G |C
They sad 'cause they in the bowl.
   |G |D7
But fish in the bowl is lucky,
   |G |C
They in for a worser fate.
    |G |D7
One day when the boss gets hungry,
    |G |
Guess who gon' be on the plate?

Chorus 2

N.C.   ‖C |G |D7 |G
Under the sea,   under the sea,
      |C |D7 |G |G7
Nobody beat us, fry us and eat us in fricas - see.
        |C |D
We what the land folks loves to cook.
      |Em |A7
Under the sea, we off the hook.
      |C |D7
We got no troubles, life is the bubbles

Chorus 3

‖C |G |D7 |G
Under the sea,   under the sea.
    |C |D7 |G |G7
Since life is sweet here, we got the beat here, natural - ly.
    |C |D |Em |A7
Even the sturgeon an' the ray, ___ they get the urge 'n start to play.
      |C |D7 |G |D7 G
We got the spirit, you got to hear it, under the sea.

Bridge

‖D7 |G
The newt play the flute. The carp play the harp.
|D7 |G
The plaice play the bass. And they soundin' sharp.
|C |G
The bass play the brass. The chub play the tub.
|D7 |G
The fluke is the duke of soul.
|D7 |G
The ray, he can play. The ling's on the strings.
|D7 |G
The trout rockin' out. The blackfish, she sings.
|C |G
The smelt and the sprat, they know where it's at.
|D7 |G   ‖
An' oh, that blowfish blow.

Interlude

```
|C          |G          |D7         |G          |
|C          |D7         |G          |G7         |
|C          |D          |Em         |A7         |
|C          |D7         |
|G          |D7  G      |           |D7   G     |
|A          |E7   A     |           |
```

                    ‖D |A |E7 |A

Chorus 4   Under the sea,   under the sea.

                          |D |E7 |A |A7
              When the sar - dine begin the be - guine, it's music to me.

                          |D |E
              What do they got, a lot of sand.

                    |F♯m |B7
              We got a hot crustacean band.

                          |D |E7 |A |E7
              Each little clam here know how to jam here under the sea.

              A |D |E7 |A |E7
              Each little slug here cuttin' a rug here under the sea.

              A |D |E
              Each little snail here know how to wail here.

                          |F♯m |B7
              That's why it's hotter under the water.

                          |D |E7
              Yeah, we in luck here down in the muck here

                          |A |E7   A | |E7 A ‖
              Under the sea.

When She Loved Me

from TOY STORY 2

Music and Lyrics by
Randy Newman

(Capo 5th fret)

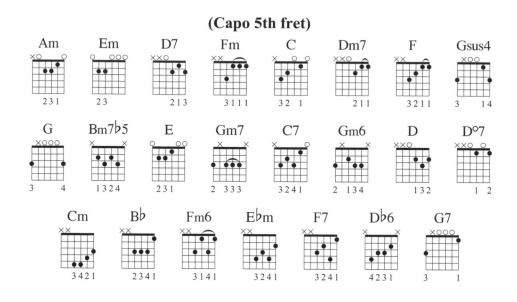

Intro

|Am   Em |D7   Fm |C | ||

Verse 1

C   Dm7 C |
When some - body loved me,

F   D7   Gsus4   G |
Ev'ry - thing was beautiful.

Bm7♭5 E   Am   C |
Ev'ry   hour we spent togeth - er

F   G ||
Lives within my heart.

Verse 2

C   Dm7 C |
And when she was sad,

F   D7   Gsus4 G |
I was there to dry her tears.

Bm7♭5 E   Am
And when she was happy,

C |F |C G7 |C ||
So was I when she loved me.

Bridge 1

F
Through the summer and the fall,
|C   Gm7 C7   F
We had each other, that was all.
 |C   F   C   D7
Just she and I to - gether,
 | G7   ‖
Like it was meant to be.

Verse 3

C   Dm7   C |
And when she was lonely,
F   D7   Gsus4 G
I was there to comfort her,
 |C7   F |C G7 |C | ‖
And I knew that she loved me.

Bridge 2

Am   Gm6 |C
So the years went by, I stayed the same.
 |D   D°7   C   Cm |
But she be - gan to drift a - way,
B♭   E   Am |
I was left a - lone.
Fm6 G   E♭m   F7 |
Still I waited for the day
               |D♭6 |E♭m G7   ‖
When she'd say, "I will always love   you."

Verse 4

C   Dm7   C |
Lonely and for - gotten,
F   D7   Gsus4 G
Never thought she'd look my way,
       |Bm7♭5 E   Am   C
And she smiled at me and held me
 |F   G
Just like she used to do,
       |C7   F |C   G7 ‖
Like she loved me when she loved me.

Outro

C   Dm7 C |
When some - body loved me,
F   D7   Gsus4 G |
Ev'ry - thing was beautiful.
Bm7♭5 E   Am   C |
Ev'ry   hour we spent togeth - er
F   G |C G7 |C | | ‖
Lives within my heart, when she loved me.

Whistle While You Work

from SNOW WHITE AND THE SEVEN DWARFS

Words by Larry Morey
Music by Frank Churchill

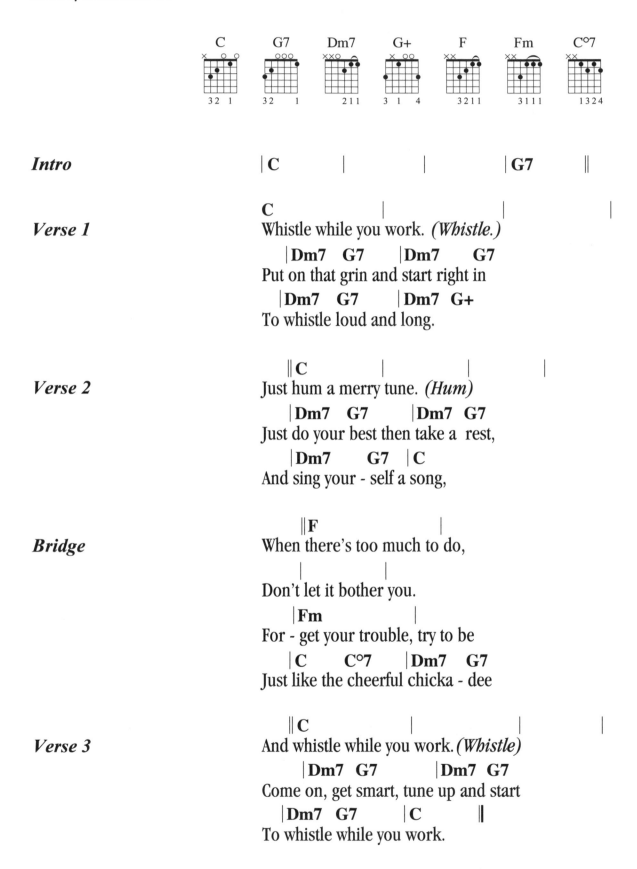

Intro | C | | | G7   ‖

Verse 1
C | | |
Whistle while you work. *(Whistle.)*
    |Dm7   G7 |Dm7   G7
Put on that grin and start right in
    |Dm7   G7 |Dm7   G+
To whistle loud and long.

Verse 2
‖ C | | |
Just hum a merry tune. *(Hum)*
    |Dm7   G7 |Dm7   G7
Just do your best then take a rest,
    |Dm7   G7 |C
And sing your - self a song,

Bridge
‖F |
When there's too much to do,
    | |
Don't let it bother you.
    |Fm |
For - get your trouble, try to be
    |C   C°7 |Dm7   G7
Just like the cheerful chicka - dee

Verse 3
‖ C | | |
And whistle while you work. *(Whistle)*
    |Dm7   G7 |Dm7   G7
Come on, get smart, tune up and start
    |Dm7   G7 |C   ‖
To whistle while you work.

Who's Afraid of the Big Bad Wolf?

from THREE LITTLE PIGS

Words and Music by Frank Churchill
Additional Lyric by Ann Ronell

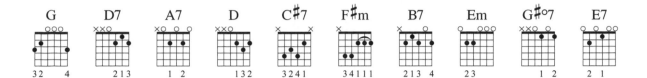

Intro

|G |D7 | |G   D7 ‖

Chorus 1

G |D7 |
Who's afraid of the big bad wolf,
          |G |
Big bad wolf, big bad wolf?
                    |D7 |
Who's afraid of the big bad wolf?
          |G   D7 |
Tra, la, la, la, la.
G |D7 |
Who's afraid of the big bad wolf,
          |G |
Big bad wolf, big bad wolf?
                    |D7 |
Who's afraid of the big bad wolf?
          |G
Tra, la, la, la, la.

Verse 1

A7   ‖D   G |D   A7
Long a - go there were three pigs,
          |D   G |D
Little handsome piggy wigs.
A7 |D |
For the big bad, very big,
G |A7 |D
Very bad wolf they didn't give three figs.

Verse 2

A7　　‖D　　G　|D　　A7
Number one was very gay,
　　　　|D　　G　　　　|D
And he built his house with hay.
A7　|D　　　　　　|G
With a hey-hey toot, he blew on his flute,
　　　　|A7　　　　　　　|D　　D7　　‖
And he played around all day.

Bridge

G　　C♯7　|F♯m　B7
Number two was fond of jigs,
　　|Em　A7　　　|D　　G♯°7　D　　　|
And so he built his house with　　twigs.
G　　　　C♯7　　|F♯m　　　　B7
Heigh diddle diddle, he played on his fiddle
　　|E7　　　　　|A7
And danced with lady pigs.

Verse 3

　　　　　‖D　　　G　　|D　A7
Number three said, "Nix on tricks.
　　|D　　G　　　　|D
I will build my house with bricks."
A7　|D　　　　　　　|G
He　had no chance to sing and dance 'cause
A7　　　　　　　　|D　　　　　　‖
Work and play don't mix!
N.C.　　　　　|　　　　　　　|
Ha, ha, ha! The two little, do little pigs
　　　　　　　　|　　　　　　　‖
Just winked and laughed ha, ha!

Chorus 2

Repeat Chorus 1

Verse 4

A7　　　‖D　　G　　|D　　A7
Come the day when fate did frown
　　　　|D　　G　|D
And the wolf blew into town.
A7　|D　　　　　　|G
With a gruff "puff, puff" he puffed just enough,
　　　|A7　　　　　　|D
And the hay　house fell right down.

Verse 5

A7   ‖D   G |D   A7
One and two were scared to death
       |D   G |D
Of the big bad wolfie's breath.
  A7 |D |G
"By the hair of your chinny-chin I'll blow you in."
      |A7 |D   D7 ‖
And the twig house answered, "yes."

Bridge 2

G   C♯7 |F♯m B7
No one left but number three
 |Em   A7 |D G♯°7 D |
To save the piglet fam - i - ly.
G   C♯7 |F♯m   B7
When they knocked, he fast un - locked
 |E7 |A7
And said, "Come in with me!"

Verse 6

        ‖D   G |D   A7
Now they all were safe in - side,
     |D   G |D
And the bricks hurt wolfie's pride.
A7 |D |G
So he slid down the chimney and, oh, by Jim'ney,
   |A7 |D   ‖
In the fire he was fried.

Interlude

N.C. | |
Ha, ha, ha! The three little, free little pigs
           | ‖
Rejoiced and laughed ha, ha!

Chorus 3

G |D7 |
Who's afraid of the big bad wolf,
      |G |
Big bad wolf, big bad wolf?
          |D7 |
Who's afraid of the big bad wolf?
      |G D7 |
Tra, la, la, la, la.
G |D7 |
Who's afraid of the big bad wolf,
      |G |
Big bad wolf, big bad wolf?
        |D7 |
Who's afraid of the big bad wolf?
      |G   ‖
Tra, la, la, la, la.

A Whole New World

from ALADDIN

Music by Alan Menken
Lyrics by Tim Rice

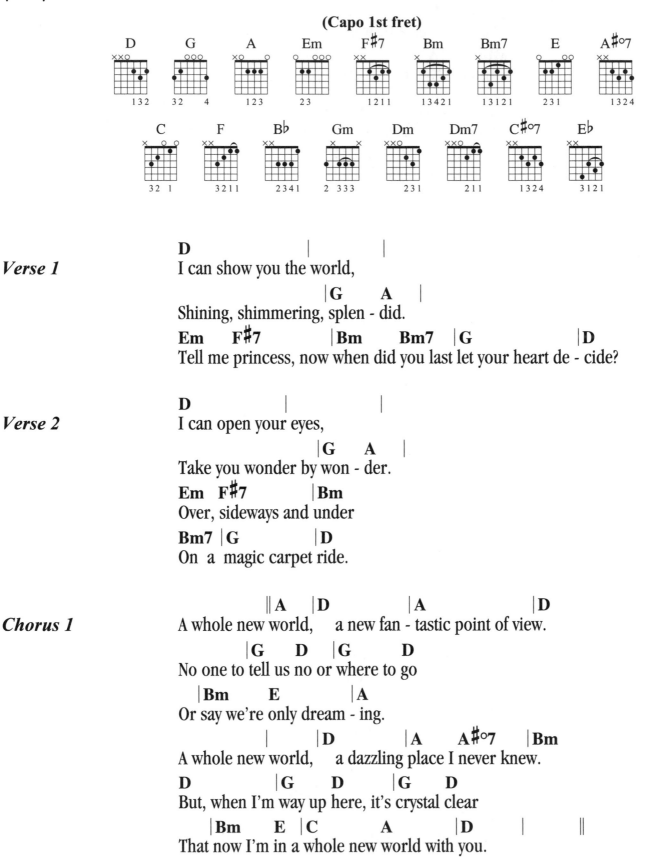

(Capo 1st fret)

Verse 1

D | | |
I can show you the world,

| **G** **A** |
Shining, shimmering, splen - did.

Em **F#7** | **Bm** **Bm7** | **G** | **D** ‖
Tell me princess, now when did you last let your heart de - cide?

Verse 2

D | | |
I can open your eyes,

| **G** **A** |
Take you wonder by won - der.

Em **F#7** | **Bm**
Over, sideways and under

Bm7 | **G** | **D**
On a magic carpet ride.

Chorus 1

‖ **A** | **D** | **A** | **D**
A whole new world, a new fan - tastic point of view.

| **G** **D** | **G** **D**
No one to tell us no or where to go

| **Bm** **E** | **A**
Or say we're only dream - ing.

| | **D** | **A** **A#°7** | **Bm**
A whole new world, a dazzling place I never knew.

D | **G** **D** | **G** **D**
But, when I'm way up here, it's crystal clear

| **Bm** **E** | **C** **A** | **D** | ‖
That now I'm in a whole new world with you.

Verse 3

```
F              |        |
Unbelievable sights,
               |Bb  C   |
Indescribable feel - ing.
Gm      A               |Dm
Soaring, tumbling, free - wheeling
Dm        |Bb             |F
Through an endless diamond sky.
```

Chorus 2

```
                 ‖C    |F         |C              |F
A whole new world,    a hundred thousand things to see.
             |Bb     F     |Bb      F
I'm like a shooting star, I've come so far,
 |Dm     G      |Bb
I can't go back to where…
                 |C          |F
A whole new world
                 |C      C#°7 |Dm
With new ho - rizons to pur - sue.
F               |Bb   F
I'll chase them any - where.
         |Bb    F       |
There's time to spare.
Dm   G        |Eb       C       |Dm        |Dm7
Let me share this whole new world with you.
```

Outro

```
                 ‖Bb
A whole new world,
F                 |Gm         |
That's where we'll be.
F        |Bb              |C
A thrilling chase. A wond'rous place
                 |F     |     |     |     ‖
For you and me.
```

Winnie the Pooh

from THE MANY ADVENTURES OF WINNIE THE POOH

Words and Music by
Richard M. Sherman and Robert B. Sherman

(Capo 5th fret)

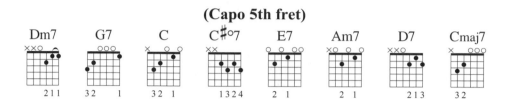

Verse 1

 Dm7 | **G7** | **C** | **C#°7**
Deep in the hundred acre wood

 | **Dm7** | **G7** | **C** | |
Where Christopher Robin plays,

 | **Dm7** | **G7** | **C** | **E7** | **Am7**
You will find the en - chanted neigh - bor - hood

 | **D7** | **G7** | **C** | | ||
Of Christopher's childhood days.

Verse 2

 || **Dm7** | **G7** | **C** | **C#°7**
A donkey named Eeyore is his friend,

 | **Dm7** | **G7** | **C**
And Kanga and little Roo.

 | **Dm7** | **G7** | **C** | **Am7**
There's Rabbit and Piglet and there's Owl,

 | **D7** | **G7** | **C** | ||
But most of all Winnie the Pooh.

Chorus

 ||: **G7** | **Cmaj7** |
 Winnie the Pooh, Winnie the Pooh.

 G7 | **C**
Tubby little cubby all stuffed with fluff.

 | **G7** | **Cmaj7** |
He's Winnie the Pooh, Winnie the Pooh.

 G7 | **C** :||
Willie, nilly, silly, ole bear.

You'll Be in My Heart

from TARZAN®

Words and Music by
Phil Collins

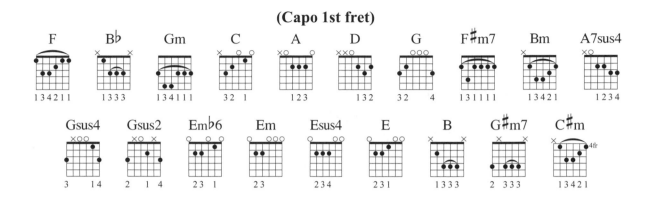

(Capo 1st fret)

Intro | F | | | ‖

Verse 1

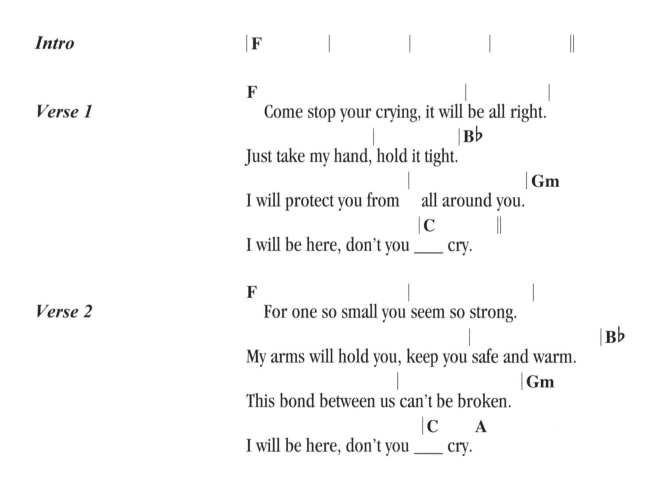

F
   Come stop your crying, it will be all right. | |

    | |**Bb**
Just take my hand, hold it tight.

        | |**Gm**
I will protect you from   all around you.

        |**C**   ‖
I will be here, don't you ___ cry.

Verse 2

F | |
   For one so small you seem so strong.

        | |**Bb**
My arms will hold you, keep you safe and warm.

        | |**Gm**
This bond between us can't be broken.

        |**C**   **A**
I will be here, don't you ___ cry.

Chorus 1

  ‖D |G
'Cause you'll be in my heart,
  |A |F♯m7
Yes, you'll be in my heart
   |Bm |G |C |A |
From this day on, now and forever - more.
D |G
You'll be in my heart
  |A |F♯m7
No matter what they say.
   |Bm |G |C |A7sus4 G |A   ‖
You'll be here in my heart al - ways.

Verse 3

   F | |
 Why can't they understand the way we feel?
            | |B♭
They just don't trust what they can't ex - plain.
            | |Gm
I know we're diff'rent, but deep inside us
        |C   A
We're not that different at all.

Chorus 2

  ‖D |G
And you'll be in my heart,
  |A |F♯m7
Yes, you'll be in my heart
   |Bm |G |C |A
From this day on, now and forever - more.

Bridge

‖Gsus4 G |Gsus2   G
Don't listen to them, 'cause what do they know?
　|Em♭6　　Em　|Esus4 Em
We need each other to have, to hold.
　　　|Bm　　　|　　|C　　　|
They'll see in time,　　I know.
　　　|Gsus4 G　　　　|Gsus2 G
When destiny calls you, you must be strong.
　|Em♭6　　Em　　　　　|Esus4　　Em
It may not be with you, but you've got to hold on.
　　|Bm　　|　　|C　　|
They'll see in time,　　I ___ know.
　　|D　　　　|A
We'll show them to - gether,

Chorus 3

　　　‖E　　　　|A
'Cause you'll be in my heart.
　　　|B　　　　|G♯m7
Believe me, you'll be in my heart.
　　　　　|C♯m　　|A　　　　　　|D　　|B　　|
I'll be there from this day on, now and forevermore.
E　　　　|A
You'll be in my heart, (You'll be here in my heart.)
　|B　　　　|G♯m7
No matter what they say, (I'll be with you.)
　|C♯m　|A　　　　　　|D　　|B
You'll be in my heart (I'll be there.) al - ways,
　|A　　|　　|E　　　|
Al - ways.　I'll be with you.
　　|A　　　　　　　　|　　　　|E　　　|
I'll be there for you always,　always and al - ways.
　　　|A　　　　|
Just look o - ver your shoulder.
　　　|E　　　　|
Just look o - ver your shoulder.
　　　|A　　　　|
Just look o - ver your shoulder,
　　　　　|E　　|　　‖
I'll be there always.

You Can Fly! You Can Fly! You Can Fly!

from PETER PAN

Words by Sammy Cahn
Music by Sammy Fain

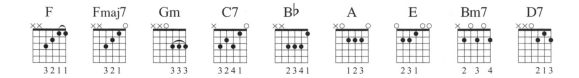

Verse 1

F |Fmaj7 |
Think of a wonderful thought,

Gm |Fmaj7 |
Any merry little thought

C7 |F |
Think of Christmas, think of snow,

C7 |F |
Think of sleigh bells, off you go!

  |B♭ | | |
Like reindeer in the sky.

C7 |F |Gm |F | ‖
You can fly! You can fly! You can fly!

Verse 2

F |Fmaj7 |
Think of the happiest things,

Gm |Fmaj7 |
It's the same as having wings.

C7 |F |
Take the path that moon beams make.

C7 |F |
If the moon is still awake,

  |B♭ | | |
You'll see him wink his eye.

C7 |F |Gm |F | ‖
You can fly! You can fly! You can fly!

Bridge

A |E
Up you go with a heigh and ho
    |A |Bm7 E
To the stars beyond the blue.
     |A |E |Bm7
There's a Neverland waiting for you
         |E |A
Where all your happy dreams come true.
   |Gm |C7 |F |C7 ||
Every dream that you dream will come true.

Verse 3

F |Fmaj7 |
When there's a smile in your heart
Gm |Fmaj7 D7 |
There's no better time to start.
C7 |F |
Think of all the joy you'll find
C7 |F
When you leave the world behind
  |Bb | | |
And bid your cares goodbye.
C7 |F |Gm |F
You can fly! You can fly! You can fly!
    |Gm |F ||
You can fly! You can fly!

You've Got a Friend in Me

from TOY STORY

Music and Lyrics by
Randy Newman

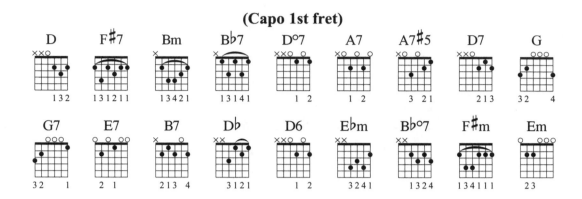

(Capo 1st fret)

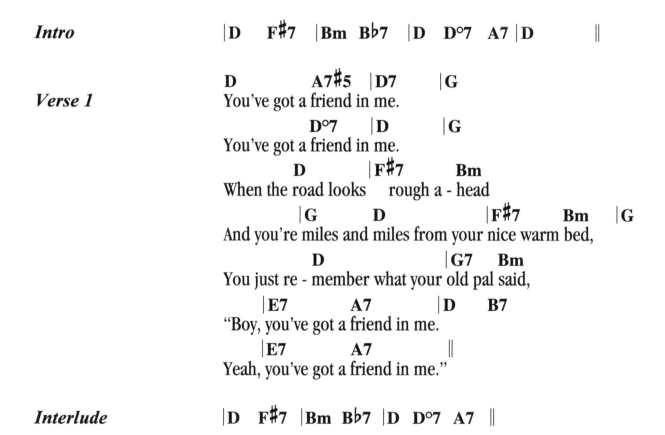

Intro |D   F#7 |Bm   Bb7 |D   D°7   A7 |D   ‖

Verse 1

D   A7#5 |D7 |G
You've got a friend in me.

        D°7 |D |G
You've got a friend in me.

        D |F#7   Bm
When the road looks   rough a - head

        |G   D |F#7   Bm |G
And you're miles and miles from your nice warm bed,

        D |G7   Bm
You just re - member what your old pal said,

|E7   A7 |D   B7
"Boy, you've got a friend in me.

|E7   A7   ‖
Yeah, you've got a friend in me."

Interlude |D   F#7 |Bm   Bb7 |D   D°7   A7 ‖

Verse 2

```
D              A7♯5  |D7        |G
You've got a friend in me.
                D°7      |D       |G
You've got a friend in me.
              D          |F♯7     Bm   |G
You got troubles, then I got 'em, too.
              D          |F♯7     Bm        |
There isn't anything I wouldn't do for you.
G             D                 |F♯7 Bm
If we stick to - gether we can see it through,
       |E7           A7          |D      B7 |E7
'Cause you've got a friend in me.
              A7         |D              ‖
You've got a friend in me.
```

Bridge

```
G                                      |D♭           |D6
      Now, some other folks might be a little smarter than I am,
       D°7           |D6         |D♭
Bigger and stronger, too. ____ Maybe.
      E♭m     |B♭°7 D♭       |F♯m B7
But none of them will ever love you the way I do,
     |Em    A7          ‖
Just me and you, boy.
```

Verse 3

```
D              A7♯5  |D7
     And as the years go by,
     |G              D°7 |D        |G
Our friendship will never die.
             D°7       |D    Bm  |E7
You're gonna see it's our desti - ny.
             A7         |D    B7  |E7
You've got a friend in me.
             A7         |D    B7  |E7
You've got a friend in me.
             A7             ‖
You've got a friend in me.
```

Outro

```
|D   F♯7 |Bm  B♭7 |D  D°7 A7 |D          ‖
```

Zip-A-Dee-Doo-Dah

from SONG OF THE SOUTH

Words by Ray Gilbert
Music by Allie Wrubel

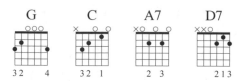

Verse 1

G   **|C**   **G** |
Zip-a-dee-doo-dah, zip-a-dee-ay,
C   **G**   **|A7**   **D7** |
My, oh my, what a wonderful day!
G   **|C**   **G** |
Plenty of sunshine, headin' my way.
C   **G**   **|A7 D7 G**
Zip-a-dee-doo - dah, zip-a-dee-ay!

Bridge 1

       ‖ **D7**   **|G**
Mister Bluebird on my shoulder.
      |A7   **|D7**
It's the truth, it's "actch'll."
N.C.   ‖
Ev'rything is "satisfactch'll."

Verse 2

G   **|C**   **G** |
Zip-a-dee-doo-dah, zip-a-dee-ay!
C   **G**   **|A7**   **D7 G**   ‖
Wonderful feeling, wonder - ful day.

Verse 3   *Repeat Verse 1*

Bridge 2   *Repeat Bridge 1*

Verse 4   *Repeat Verse 2*

STRUM & SING

Lyrics, chord symbols, and guitar chord diagrams for your favorite songs.

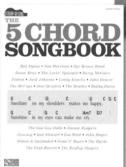

GUITAR

ACOUSTIC CLASSICS
00191891.............$12.99

ADELE
00159855.............$12.99

SARA BAREILLES
00102354.............$12.99

THE BEATLES
00172234.............$16.99

BLUES
00159335.............$12.99

ZAC BROWN BAND
02501620.............$12.99

COLBIE CAILLAT
02501725.............$14.99

CAMPFIRE FOLK SONGS
02500686.............$12.99

CHART HITS OF 2014-2015
00142554.............$12.99

CHART HITS OF 2015-2016
00156248.............$12.99

BEST OF KENNY CHESNEY
00142457.............$14.99

CHRISTMAS SONGS
00171332.............$14.99

KELLY CLARKSON
00146384.............$14.99

JOHN DENVER COLLECTION
02500632.............$9.95

EAGLES
00157994.............$12.99

EASY ACOUSTIC SONGS
00125478.............$14.99

50 CHILDREN'S SONGS
02500825.............$9.99

THE 5 CHORD SONGBOOK
02501718.............$12.99

FOLK SONGS
02501482.............$10.99

FOLK/ROCK FAVORITES
02501669.............$10.99

THE 4 CHORD SONGBOOK
02501533.............$12.99

THE 4-CHORD COUNTRY SONGBOOK
00114936.............$14.99

THE GREATEST SHOWMAN
00278383.............$14.99

HAMILTON
00217116.............$14.99

HITS OF THE '70S
02500871.............$9.99

HYMNS
02501125.............$8.99

JACK JOHNSON
02500858.............$16.99

ROBERT JOHNSON
00191890.............$12.99

CAROLE KING
00115243.............$10.99

BEST OF GORDON LIGHTFOOT
00139393.............$14.99

DAVE MATTHEWS BAND
02501078.............$10.95

JOHN MAYER
02501636.............$10.99

INGRID MICHAELSON
02501634.............$10.99

THE MOST REQUESTED SONGS
02501748.............$12.99

JASON MRAZ
02501452.............$14.99

PRAISE & WORSHIP
00152381.............$12.99

ELVIS PRESLEY
00198890.............$12.99

QUEEN
00218578.............$12.99

ROCK AROUND THE CLOCK
00103625.............$12.99

ROCK BALLADS
02500872.............$9.95

ED SHEERAN
00152016.............$14.99

THE 6 CHORD SONGBOOK
02502277.............$10.99

CAT STEVENS
00116827.............$14.99

TAYLOR SWIFT
00159856.............$12.99

THE 3 CHORD SONGBOOK
00211634.............$9.99

TODAY'S HITS
00119301.............$12.99

TOP CHRISTIAN HITS
00156331.............$12.99

TOP HITS OF 2016
00194288.............$12.99

KEITH URBAN
00118558.............$14.99

THE WHO
00103667.............$12.99

NEIL YOUNG – GREATEST HITS
00138270.............$14.99

UKULELE

THE BEATLES
00233899.............$16.99

COLBIE CAILLAT
02501731.............$10.99

JOHN DENVER
02501694.............$10.99

FOLK ROCK FAVORITES FOR UKULELE
00114600.............$9.99

THE 4-CHORD UKULELE SONGBOOK
00114331.............$14.99

JACK JOHNSON
02501702.............$17.99

JOHN MAYER
02501706.............$10.99

INGRID MICHAELSON
02501741.............$12.99

THE MOST REQUESTED SONGS
02501453.............$14.99

JASON MRAZ
02501753.............$14.99

SING-ALONG SONGS
02501710.............$15.99

HAL•LEONARD®

www.halleonard.com
Visit our website to see full song lists.

Prices, content, and availability subject to change without notice.